Materials

These two pages show the variety of art materials that are used in the papercraft projects in this book.

Paper ideas

Below are some of the different papers that are used for the projects. Beneath the heading on most of the pages you'll find a suggestion for the kind of paper to use for that project.

Using a craft knife

Some of the projects suggest using a craft knife to cut out shapes. When you use one, always put a pile of old magazines or one or two pieces of thick cardboard under the paper you are cutting.

Be very careful when you use a craft knife. Keep your fingers away from the blade.

This pink paper has been textured with paint (see pages 6-9).

Patterned wrapping paper

Pages ripped from old magazines

Tissue paper

Corrugated cardboard from an old box. Rip off the top layer of paper to reveal the bumpy surface.

Corrugated cardboard from an art shop

Paper with a raised texture

Art paper is thick and is usually sold in individual sheets.

Scraps of shiny paper from packaging or wrapping paper

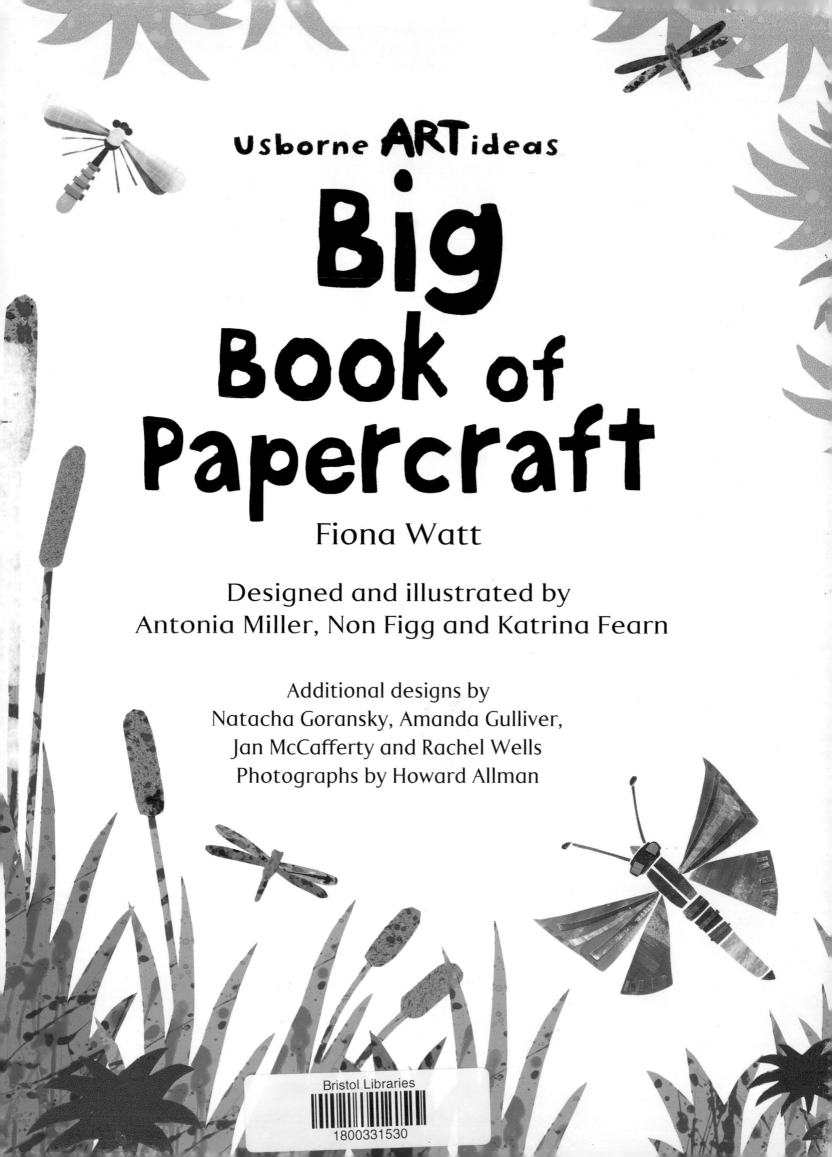

Usborne ART ideas

Big
Book of
Papercraft

Fiona Watt

Designed and illustrated by
Antonia Miller, Non Figg and Katrina Fearn

Additional designs by
Natacha Goransky, Amanda Gulliver,
Jan McCafferty and Rachel Wells
Photographs by Howard Allman

Contents

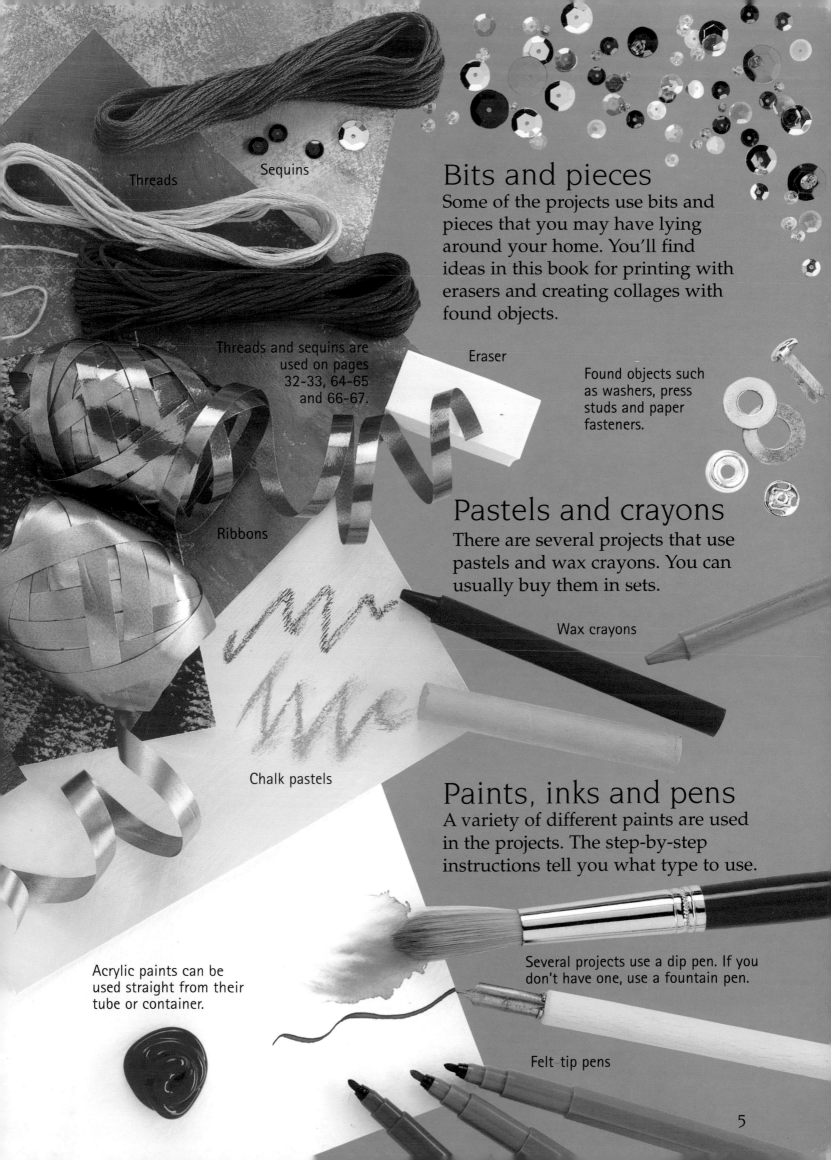

Threads

Sequins

Bits and pieces
Some of the projects use bits and pieces that you may have lying around your home. You'll find ideas in this book for printing with erasers and creating collages with found objects.

Threads and sequins are used on pages 32-33, 64-65 and 66-67.

Eraser

Found objects such as washers, press studs and paper fasteners.

Ribbons

Pastels and crayons
There are several projects that use pastels and wax crayons. You can usually buy them in sets.

Wax crayons

Chalk pastels

Paints, inks and pens
A variety of different paints are used in the projects. The step-by-step instructions tell you what type to use.

Acrylic paints can be used straight from their tube or container.

Several projects use a dip pen. If you don't have one, use a fountain pen.

Felt tip pens

5

Creating textured paper

Several of the projects in this book, including the paper weaving on pages 28-29 and the 3-D bugs on pages 60-61, use pieces of paper which have been textured by using different paint techniques.

Experiment with the examples on the following four pages to create your own papers.

Wax resist

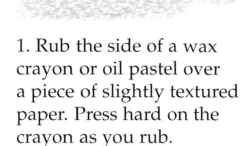

1. Rub the side of a wax crayon or oil pastel over a piece of slightly textured paper. Press hard on the crayon as you rub.

2. Mix some water with paint and brush it over the paper. The wax will resist the paint, leaving the texture of the paper.

Brushmarks

1. Dip a thick household paintbrush in yellow paint, then brush it in stripes across a piece of white paper.

2. Mix some red with the yellow to make orange. Brush it lightly across the yellow paint so that you leave brushmarks.

3. While the paint is still wet, brush red paint on top of the yellow and orange paint, leaving marks as before.

These papers have been textured using the techniques shown above.

Swirly circles

1. Dip a dry, broad paintbrush into thick acrylic paint so that the paint just covers the tips of the bristles.

2. Brush the paint around and around on a piece of paper, pressing hard. You should get lots of individual brushmarks.

3. Dip the tips of the bristles into the paint again and brush another circle beside the first one. Do this again and again.

Sponge marks

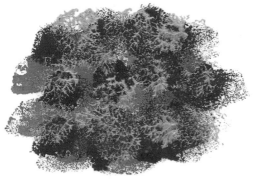

1. Dip a piece of sponge into some paint, then dab it onto a piece of paper. Dip it into the paint each time you dab it on.

2. Then, dab a darker shade of paint over the top of it, leaving some of the original paint showing through.

3. You can even sponge a third shade on top, or dab on some gold or silver acrylic paint, if you have some.

The paper below has been textured by sponging blue paint onto white paper.

More texturing ideas

These pages give you some more examples of how you can create textured papers to use in your projects.

This paper was created by dropping blobs of ink onto wet paper.

This rubbing was done with yellow wax crayon on the large holes of a cheese grater. The rubbing was then painted with ink.

This rubbing was done on the small holes on a cheese grater.

For this effect, sprinkle salt onto wet watery paint. Let it dry, then rub off all the salt.

Paint a piece of plastic foodwrap with paint. Lay a piece of paper on top. Rub lightly over the paper, then lift it off.

This background was also
done with paint on plastic
foodwrap (see below left).

These pieces were painted with a
household paintbrush. Paint on
one shade of paint, then brush
another shade on top when dry.

This paper was
painted with watery
paints. It was then
spattered with clean
water while the
paint was wet. Pages
30-31 show you
how to spatter.

Rub the side of a wax crayon
over a piece of paper then
paint it all over.

Textured paper picture

BLACK PAPER AND SMALL PIECES OF WHITE PAPER

The steps on this page show you different ways of making textured paper and patterns with paint, pastels and collage. You don't need to follow the ideas exactly, just experiment with the different techniques. You could then cut your samples into squares and then glue them together to make a picture.

1. Follow the steps on page 7 to paint a swirly circle with light blue or ultramarine paint. Use a thick paintbrush.

2. Paint another piece of paper with blue paint. When it's dry, cut it into strips and glue them onto a piece of white paper.

3. Use a chalk pastel or oil pastel to scribble thick lines across a piece of paper. Do it quickly and don't try to be too neat.

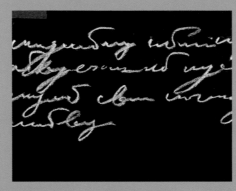

4. Use a white chalk pastel to write long lines of flowing, joined-up writing across a piece of black paper.

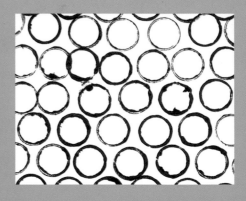

5. Spread black paint on an old saucer, then dip a bottle top into it. Use the bottle top to print several rows of circles.

6. Paint two blue lines across some paper. Glue on two strips which have been painted with black paint. Add a pink square.

7. Use paint to fill in blocks of blue on a piece of paper. Use a chalk pastel to draw a white line across the middle.

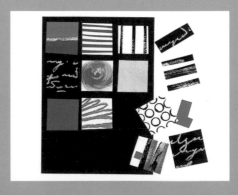

8. Cut the pieces of textured paper into rough squares. Arrange them on a large piece of black paper, then glue them on.

Tissue paper flowers

TISSUE PAPER AND THICK PAPER

1. Rip some strips of blue tissue paper. Glue them across a piece of paper, making them overlap.

2. Cut some thin strips of green tissue paper for the stems and glue them at the bottom of the paper.

3. Cut out some red petals. Glue four petals around the top of some of the stems.

4. Cut out some orange petals. Glue them around other stems, overlapping some of the red petals.

5. Use a thin felt-tip pen to draw a line around each petal. It doesn't need to be too accurate.

6. Draw a small circle in the middle of each flower, then add two or three lines to each petal.

These flowers also have outlines drawn along their stems.

Textured houses

THIN WHITE CARDBOARD

1. Cut a zigzag at one end of a strip of cardboard. Then, paint a rectangle of acrylic paint on another piece of cardboard.

2. Drag the zigzag end of the cardboard across the paint again and again to make textured lines. Leave the paint to dry.

3. Cut several small triangles into the end of another cardboard strip. Drag it across another rectangle of paint.

4. For a very fine texture, drag the end of an old toothbrush across a rectangle of paint, again and again.

5. Do some more textured patches of paint by experimenting with different shapes cut into strips of cardboard.

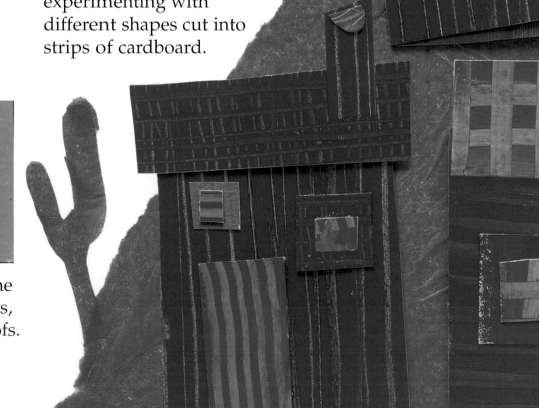

6. Cut rectangles from the textures for the buildings, windows, doors and roofs. Glue them on another piece of cardboard.

The orange strips woven through this star were cut in different widths.

5. To fill the top of the heart, cut four short strips of paper. Weave them at a slight angle, like this.

6. When the heart is completely filled, trim the ends off the strips, a little way away from the edges of the heart.

Spattered paper collage

BRIGHT PAPER, SUCH AS ART PAPER

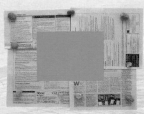

Weight the newspaper with small stones.

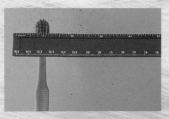

1. This can be quite messy so do this outdoors. Put your paper onto some newspapers.

2. Put some ready-mix paint into a container. Add water to make it runny.

3. Dip an old toothbrush into the paint. Then, hold the brush over the paper.

4. Pull a ruler along the brush towards you, so the paint spatters onto the paper.

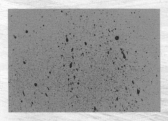

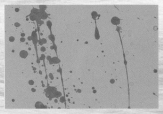

5. Keep spattering more paint on top until you get the effect you want. Let it dry.

6. Mix another shade of paint and spatter it in the same way on top of the first one.

7. To get big spatters, dip a household paintbrush into runny paint.

8. Flick the brush sharply downwards over the paper. Repeat with more paint.

9. Continue flicking the paint until you have the pattern you want. Leave it to dry.

10. Draw the outline of a frog and leaves on the back of the spattered paper.

11. Draw some plants and a strip for water on the finely spattered paper.

12. Cut out the paper shapes and glue them onto a piece of contrasting paper.

Sparkling squares

TRANSPARENT BOOK COVERING FILM

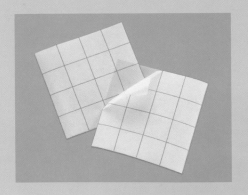

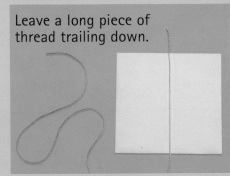

Leave a long piece of thread trailing down.

1. Cut two squares of book covering film, the same size. Peel the backing paper off one of them and lay it sticky-side up.

2. Cut a long piece of bright thread and lay it across the film, like this. It will stick to the sticky surface.

The shapes sparkle as they turn.

3. Rip lots of small pieces of tissue paper. Then, press them onto the film, leaving spaces in between them.

4. Press different shapes of sequins into the gaps between the paper. You could add some pieces of ribbon or thread, too.

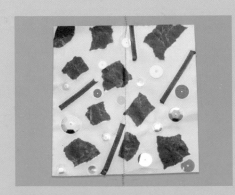

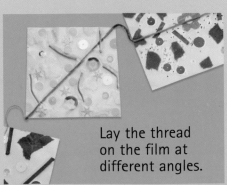

Lay the thread on the film at different angles.

5. Peel the backing paper off the other piece of film and press it over the decorated piece. Then, trim the edges.

6. Attach more squares of book film below the first one, leaving some thread showing between the squares.

These squares
of film were
stitched together.

You could add
glitter for some
extra sparkle.

33

Fashion cut-outs

ART PAPER AND WRAPPING PAPER

1. Cut out a page from an old magazine with a photograph or drawing of a figure wearing an outfit.

2. Trace a simple outline of the head, body and clothes. Then, turn the tracing over and scribble pencil over the lines.

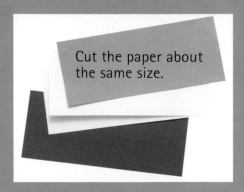

Cut the paper about the same size.

3. Cut two pieces of white paper, one brown piece and one pink. Make them larger than your figure drawing.

Press firmly.

4. Lay the tracing, shaded-side down, onto the brown paper. Draw around the head, feet and hand with a ballpoint pen.

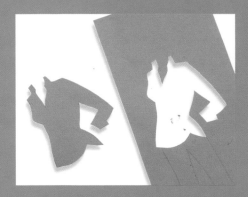

5. Cut them out with a craft knife, keeping all the shapes. Trace the clothes onto the pink paper and cut them out.

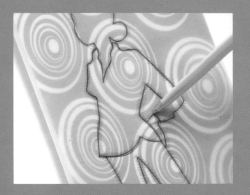

6. Lay your tracing onto a piece of wrapping paper. Draw around the clothes again, then cut them out.

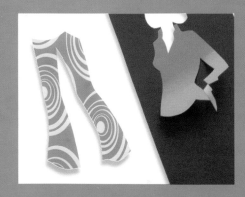

7. Glue the large piece of brown paper onto one of the pieces of white paper. Glue the pink shirt and patterned bottoms on top.

8. Glue the patterned shirt onto the other piece of white paper. Then, glue the large piece of pink paper on top.

9. Then, glue the brown head, hand and feet onto the figure on the pink paper. (You don't use the pink bottoms at all).

Glue your pictures side by side
on a large piece of paper.

If you can't find
a suitable picture
in a magazine,
trace over one
of these figures.

Folded dyed paper

WHITE OR LIGHT SHADES OF TISSUE PAPER

1. Fold a rectangle of tissue paper about the size of this page in half. Then, fold it in half three more times.

2. Dip a paintbrush in clean water and paint it all over the folded paper. Do this again and again until the paper is damp.

3. Paint a band of blue ink across the middle of the paper. Do this two or three times so that the ink soaks into the paper.

The paper below had blobs of ink painted all over it when it was folded.

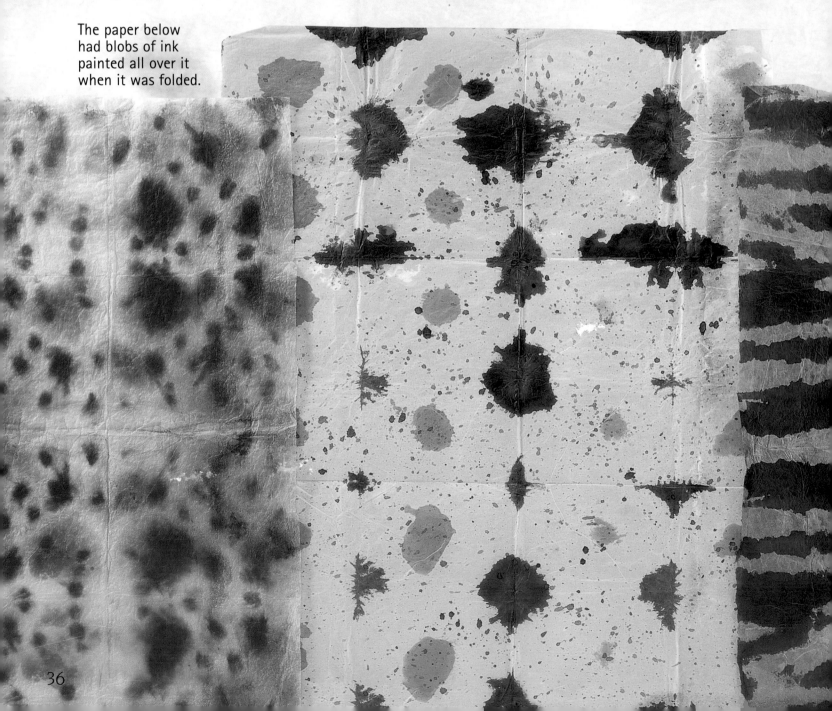

4. Paint each corner of the folded paper with purple ink. Let the ink soak into the paper and mix with the blue ink.

5. Leave the folded paper to dry. When it is completely dry, unfold it very carefully to reveal the dyed pattern.

6. Dip a paintbrush into purple ink. Hold it above the paper and flick the bristles of the brush to splatter the ink all over.

This green paper had lots of stripes painted across it.

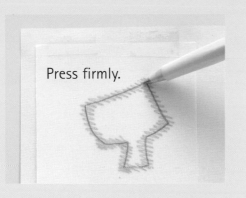

Press firmly.

Add other details, like a teddy bear.

4. Turn the tracing back over. Lay it on top of some paper with a skin tone. Draw over the face again, then cut it out.

5. Glue the face on the hair. Cut out a mouth and ear, then draw eyes and a nose. Cut a dress from textured paper and glue it on.

6. Cut out legs, arms and a pair of shoes and glue them on. Add a sleeve at the top of the arm and a heart-shaped pocket.

Tissue paper fish

TISSUE PAPER

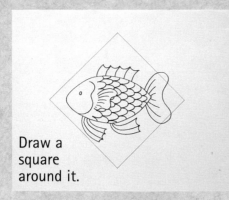

Draw a square around it.

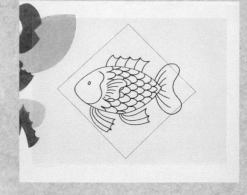

1. Use a thick black felt-tip pen to draw a bold drawing of a fish. Do it on white paper.

2. Trace the main shapes of your fish onto different shades of tissue paper, then cut them out.

Use your picture as a guide.

3. Cut a piece of polythene from a clear plastic bag. Make sure it is bigger than your drawing.

4. Lay the polythene over your drawing. Put pieces of tape along the edges to secure it.

5. Brush the tissue paper shapes with white glue. Press each one in place onto the polythene.

6. Cut or tear strips of tissue paper for the background. Glue them on around the fish.

7. Glue a piece of pale blue tissue paper over the whole picture, then leave it to dry.

8. When the glue is completely dry, carefully peel the tissue paper off the polythene.

9. Place the tissue paper over your drawing. Go over your outlines using black paint.

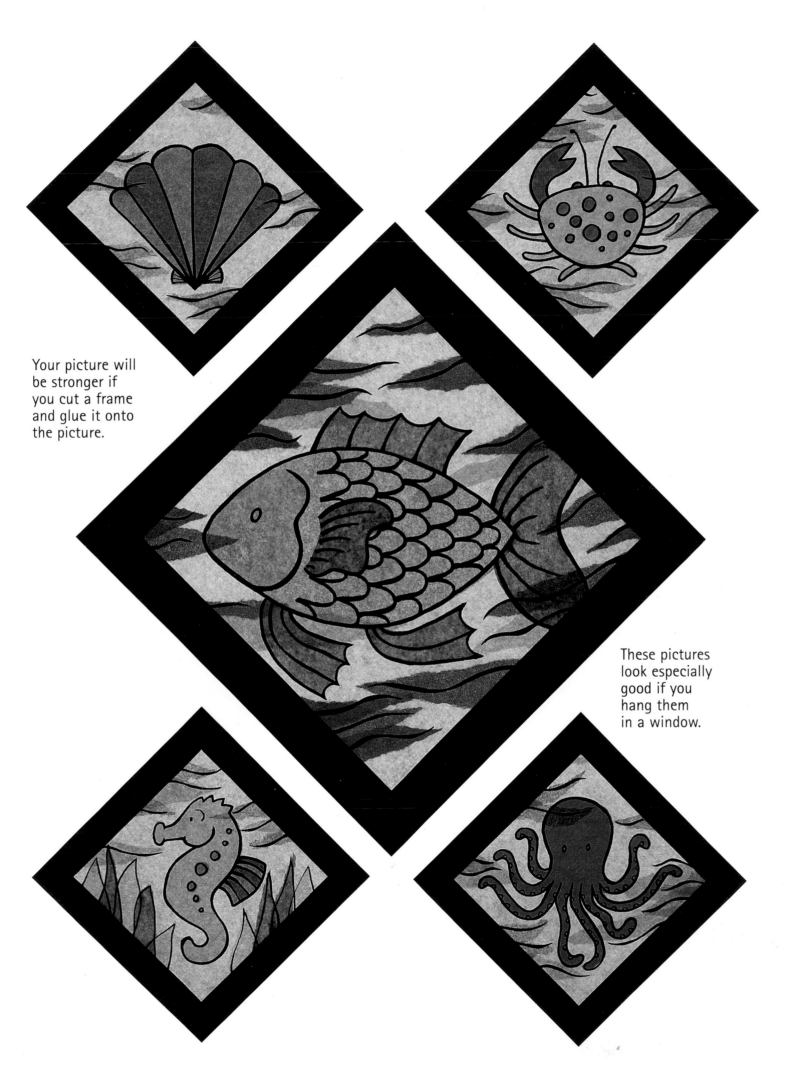

Your picture will be stronger if you cut a frame and glue it onto the picture.

These pictures look especially good if you hang them in a window.

Making frames

On the next four pages you can find out how to make different types of frames for your pictures.

When you make a frame, choose a piece of cardboard which will go well with the picture you are framing. If you decide to decorate your frame, don't make it too elaborate, otherwise your picture will be swamped.

This simple frame was made from strips of corrugated cardboard.

Simple strip frame

1. Cut a piece of cardboard the size you want your frame to be. Glue your picture in the middle of it.

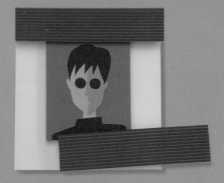

2. Cut two strips of cardboard for the top and bottom of the frame. Make sure they overlap your picture a little.

3. For the sides of the frame, cut two pieces of cardboard which fit between the top and bottom strips.

4. Glue on the top strip of cardboard, then the two sides and finally the bottom strip to complete the frame.

It's often a good idea to leave a plain border between the edge of your picture and the frame.

A square 'window' frame

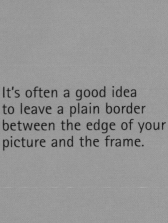

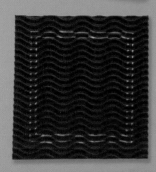

1. Cut two squares of cardboard the size you want the frame. Then, lay your picture on one of the squares.

2. Use a pencil to draw around your picture. This will give you a guide for the size for the 'window' you'll cut into the frame.

3. Draw another shape about 5mm (¼ in.) inside the pencil lines. Then, place the cardboard on an old magazine.

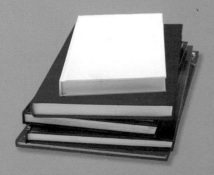

4. Cut along the inside shape with a craft knife. Cut each line several times rather than trying to cut through first time.

5. Lay the frame over your picture. Turn them over and attach the picture with pieces of tape. Then, erase any pencil lines.

6. Glue the frame onto the spare cardboard square. Put a heavy pile of books on top until the glue has dried.

More frame ideas

These two pages show ideas for decorating the strip frame and window frame shown on the previous two pages.

Glue lots of pieces of ripped tissue paper to make a frame like this orangey-red one.

The picture it is framing had lines painted with acrylic paint. Then, chalk pastel patterns were added when the paint was dry.

This corrugated cardboard frame was cut from an old box. It was painted with acrylic paint, then rubbed with sandpaper when the paint was dry.

The line around the window was drawn with a gold felt-tip pen.

This picture is a cardboard collage (see pages 18-19).

The strip frame above was made from a foil food tray. The patterns were drawn on the back with a ballpoint pen.

The middle frame was decorated with squares cut from pieces of textured paper (see pages 6-9).

The bottom frame was made using a foil food tray and decorated with squares of textured paper.

Ideas for hanging pictures

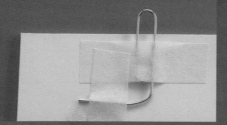

Bend this side upwards.

For a loop hanger, cut a piece of thin string and use a piece of strong tape to attach it to the back of your frame.

For a metal hanger, unbend the end of a paperclip. Use several pieces of strong tape to attach it to the frame.

To make a stand, cut a triangle from cardboard and fold it in half. Cut the bottom edges at an angle, then glue on one half.

Simple figures

THICK BRIGHT PAPER OR CARDBOARD

1. Cut a piece of thick paper or cardboard. Rip a rectangle from some brown wrapping paper and glue it in the middle.

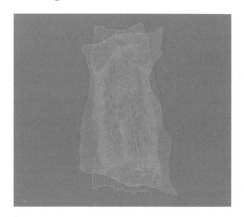

2. Rip a slightly wider rectangle from a bright piece of tissue paper and glue it over the brown wrapping paper.

3. When the glue has dried, use a water-based felt-tip pen or a fountain pen to draw an oval for the face.

4. Draw two lines for the neck and a round-necked T-shirt. Add lines for the arms, but don't worry about drawing hands.

5. Draw a curved line for the eyebrow and nose, then add the other eyebrow and eyes. Draw the ears, hair and lips.

6. Then, dip a paintbrush into some clean water. Paint the water along some of the lines to make the ink run a little.

7. Rip a rough T-shirt shape from tissue paper and glue it over your drawing. Add a torn paper stripe, too.

8. Finally, when the glue has dried, paint thin stripes across the T-shirt using a bright shade of watery paint.

59

3-D bugs

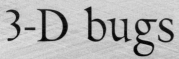

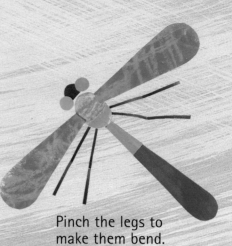

Pinch the legs to make them bend.

1. Cut out the middle and lower parts of a bug's body from textured paper. Glue the pieces onto some thick paper or cardboard.

2. Cut out a dome-shaped head and two eyes, and glue them on. Also cut out and glue on yellow shapes to fit on the body.

3. Cut out and glue on two lower wings. Cut four legs. Glue on the ends nearest the body. Pinch them in the middle.

The bug below is the one described in the steps.

Pull the folded ends out to make it stand up.

4. Cut out two more wings from tracing paper or tissue paper. Pinch each narrow end to make a fold. Glue on that end only.

5. For the ridges down the body, cut a strip of paper. Fold each end inward, then fold the ends back on themselves.

This orange bug has three sets of wings cut from textured paper.

Dangling Christmas trees

WRAPPING PAPER

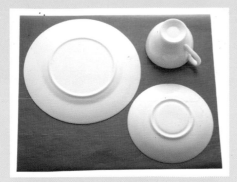

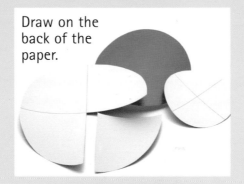

Draw on the back of the paper.

Cut about halfway up the cone.

1. Draw around three circular objects of different sizes on a piece of wrapping paper. Then, cut out the circles.

2. Roughly divide each circle into quarters, then cut a quarter from each one. You don't need the quarters you have cut out.

3. Bend the largest circle around to make a cone and glue it together. Then, make lots of cuts around the bottom edge.

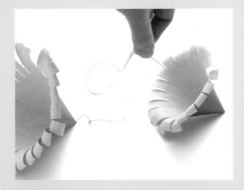

4. Roll each strip you have cut around a pencil, to make it curl. Make cones from the other two circles. Cut and curl them, too.

5. Thread a needle onto a long piece of thread. Make a big knot in one end. Push the needle up through the big cone.

6. Push the cone down as far as the knot. Make another knot a little further up the thread, then add the middle cone.

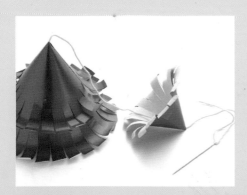

7. Push the middle cone down onto the second knot. Then, make a final knot and thread the smallest cone onto it.

8. Press a star sticker on either side of the thread at the top of the tree, or cut out and glue on stars or large flat sequins.

9. If you have used plain wrapping paper, you could decorate the trees with dots of glitter glue or tiny stickers.

Foil fish

THICK PAPER AND KITCHEN FOIL

The drops of water and the salt make the ink spread.

1. For the sea, mix turquoise ink with water, then use a thick brush to paint it all over a piece of thick paper.

2. Use the tip of the brush to dab on undiluted ink, then drop blobs of water onto it. Sprinkle salt all over, then let it dry.

3. For the sky, mix even more water with the turquoise ink and paint it all over another piece of thick paper.

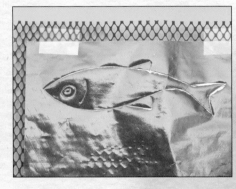

4. While the sky is still wet, dab on darker ink in a few places. Then, dab it with a tissue to lift off some of the ink.

5. While the backgrounds are drying, draw a simple fish shape on a piece of kitchen foil. Tape it to a net vegetable bag.

6. Use your thumbnail to rub the foil, inside the outline of the fish. The pattern of the net will show on the foil.

Leave the foil taped to the net.

For the best effect, use felt-tip pens with permanent ink.

7. Fill in a stripe of green felt-tip pen along the back of the fish. Add a light green stripe under it, then fill in below with yellow.

8. Draw purple and orange lines on the head. Add an eye with a black pen. Cut out the fish, then make several more.

9. Brush the salt off the sea, then cut a wavy line across it. Glue the sea onto the sky, then add the fish on top.

The salt reacts with the ink to leave these watery patterns.

Collage book covers

ANY TYPE OF PAPER

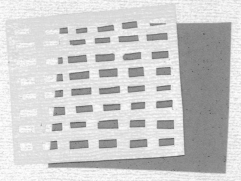 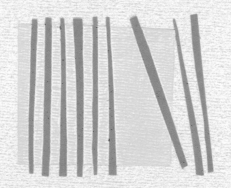 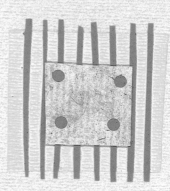

1. Use a craft knife to cut rows of little rectangles into a square of cream paper. Glue it onto a square of darker paper.

2. Then, use scissors to cut lots of thin strips of light brown paper and glue them onto a square of cream paper.

3. Use a hole puncher to punch holes into a paper square. Glue it onto brown paper, then glue them both on top of the strips.

The cream paper used in these squares is wallpaper.

Trim here. ———

4. Cut a 'spiral' in a paper square. Glue it at an angle onto some darker paper. Then, trim off any paper which overlaps the edge.

You could use these for the cover of a diary or photo album.

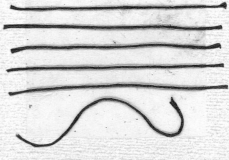

5. Cut several pieces of thick thread. Paint them with white glue, then press them in lines across a paper square.

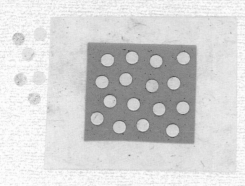

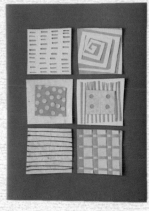

6. Decorate another square with circles from a hole puncher. Then, decorate one more using the ideas shown below.

7. Cut a piece of paper to the height of the book you want to cover. Make it long enough to fold inside the cover.

8. Lay the decorated squares in the middle of the book cover. Glue them on with strong glue, then leave it to dry.

More ideas

Include a square from a scrap of handmade paper, if you have any.

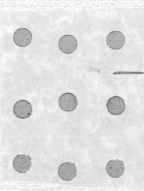

Fold some paper several times, then punch lines of holes in it.

Cut squares of different sizes and glue them on top of each other.

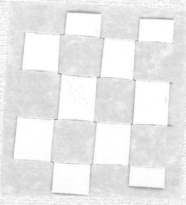

Add a small piece of paper weaving (see pages 26-27).

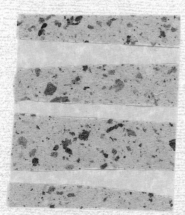

Cut strips of patterned paper and glue them on.

Rip strips of paper and glue them on top of each other.

Glue on lots of little paper squares at different angles.

Pierce lots of holes with an old ballpoint pen or a blunt needle.

3-D cityscape

THIN WHITE CARDBOARD

Make them roughly
the same width.

1. For the buildings, cut rectangles of patterned paper from magazines. Glue them onto a strip of thin white cardboard.

2. Cut out and glue on a roof for each building. Make some of them pointed and others flat on top.

3. Cut out windows, chimneys and doors, and glue them on. Try to find paper with squared or lined patterns on them.

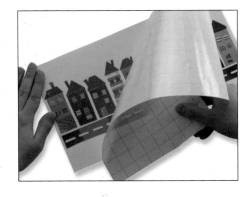

4. For the road, cut strips of blue shades of paper. Glue them on in front of the buildings. Add white lines, too.

5. To protect your collage and make it stronger, you could cover it with clear book covering film, but you don't have to.

6. Use a craft knife to cut around the buildings and the road. Leave a border of white cardboard around them.

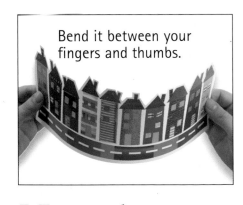

Bend it between your fingers and thumbs.

7. To curve the street so that it stands up, hold it in the middle. Move your hands outwards, bending it slightly as you go.

8. Make more streets in the same way. Make one without a road in front, then others which are taller than the first street.

9. Cut out metallic-looking papers for skyscrapers. Make them from several pieces of paper glued on top of each other.

Finish the cityscape with a road and hedges.

Assemble the streets one behind the other. You could press a small piece of poster tack on the back to secure them.

81

Index